INSTRUCTOR'S MANUAL

Second Edition

The Process of Composition

JOY M. REID
Colorado State University

PRENTICE HALL REGENTS, Englewood Cliffs, NJ 07632

10   9   8   7   6   5   4   3   2

ISBN: 0-13-723073-7

Printed in the United States of America

CONTENTS

Acknowledgements

My thanks to the teachers in the Intensive English Program
at Colorado State University, especially to Linda Stratton, for
contributions to this Teacher's Manual.

INTRODUCTION

This Teacher's Manual to The Process of Composition (POC) is designed to provide a basic syllabus that will review basic writing skills, keep the students writing and revising work, and foster in the students a sense of confidence in their ability to do competent academic work. Please read the Preface in the textbook for a more complete explanation of the philosophy behind POC.

General Operating Procedures

1. Encourage students to buy a spiral notebook in which all writing will be kept. In this way:

    A. both you and the students will be able to see their progress at a glance;
    B. students can keep all of their writing together;
    C. revisions of writing can easily be made and corrected;
    D. neither the teacher nor the students have to struggle with mounds of easily misplaced papers.

2. Hold individual conferences with students at least twice during the semester, once near the beginning to discuss the students' specific writing problems, and once near the end, to discuss any difficulties they are having with their research papers.

3. Revision of work is essential; to that end, have the students write on only one side of the page, reserving the back of each page for revisions. All revisions should be marked, perhaps graded, in order to motivate students. Students need to be encouraged to revise; research with both native and non-native speakers of English indicates that students learn as much, if not more, from revising their writing as they do from writing their final drafts.

4. Methods of presenting material can be varied and should reflect approaches used in academic classes:

    A. lectures (students take notes)
    B. class discussion
    C. small group activities and/or mini-conferencing by the teacher
    D. presentations by individual students
    E. paired activities (peer evaluation) and collaborative learning

5. The students must make the class relevant to their interests:

    A. by choosing their own topics (i.e., writing about what they know, and reading about what they don't);

        B.   by discovering the types of writing re-
              quired in their academic classes, and by
              practicing those formats in class;
        C.   by experimenting with and discovering what
              composing and revising strategies work best
              for them in different writing tasks.

The syllabus suggestions that follow have proved useful to teachers of this course. Included are suggestions for presenting textbook material, answers to some of the more difficult exercises, solutions to possible problems, and additional exercises.

Generally speaking, POC is a text for a one-semester course. The book is divided into thirds: review of paragraph skills, an extensive section on the essay, and the processes involved in writing a research paper. Please note that:

1.   the material on the inside front and back cover of POC is information that the students should use throughout their writing tasks; you might want to explain to the students that the composing and revising processes on the inside covers are deliberately NOT numbered because the writing process is complex, recursive, and individual. It will be the students' responsibility during the semester to become familiar with their individual processes as they use the inside covers.

2.   the final chapter of POC, Grammatical Explanations and Exercises, may be used for individual or class remediation throughout the course.

CHAPTER 1:   THE FUNDAMENTALS OF WRITING

After the initial procedures of the first class, you might question the students (or have the students interview each other in a paired activity) about such information as major fields, native countries, graduate or undergraduate, interests, etc. You will find such information useful in organizing the course, particularly the research paper assignment, and the students need to know their peers who will be their audience and, at times, their evaluators. Another way to learn about the students is to begin the class with a study of resumes and the business letter (see the appendix of the text).

Pre-testing

A writing sample to determine each student's strengths and weaknesses is necessary. The assignment may be completed in class or taken home; the students should spend approximately 30 minutes writing. The samples will provide you with information about:

1.   the ability to address a given topic
2.   the ability to address an academic audience appropriately
3.   weaknesses and strengths in organization, grammar, and support

Sample assignments:
1.   Write a paragraph about your mother.
2.   Select one corporation which is very successful in your country; discuss why this company is successful.
3.   Compare and contrast shopping for food in your country with shopping for food in the U.S.

You might evaluate the writing sample according to the Placement Guide below in three basic areas: English structure, content, and organization.

ENGLISH STRUCTURE

Excellent: Few noticeable errors in grammar, word order, punctuation, and/or spelling; frequent use of complex sentence structures.

Above Average: Occasional errors in grammar, word order, punctuation, and/or spelling; some use of complex sentence structures.

Average: Moderate errors in grammar, word order, punctuation, and/or spelling; general use of simple sentences; occasionally an obscured meaning.

Fair: Frequent errors in grammar, word order, punctuation, and/or spelling make comprehension difficult; use of short, basic sentence structures.

Poor: General use of phrases and/or fragments; very basic vocabulary and/or rampant misspelling.

CONTENT

Excellent: Writing is an easy task; quantity is no problem; diction is broad and appropriate; interesting, substantial, complex ideas that respond directly and completely to the assignment; topic developed fully and coherently.

Above Average: Writing flows without much hesitation; reasonable quantity; some diction errors of complex words; interesting ideas that are relevant to the assignment; ideas develop the topic with specific detail and coherence.

Average: Evidence of having stopped writing at times; somewhat limited vocabulary; adequate development of ideas relevant to the assignment with some specific detail; flawed coherence.

Fair: Limited quantity; limited development; little specific detail; simple ideas not necessarily related to the assignment; simple vocabulary with frequent diction errors.

Poor: Little writing; very simple ideas, often not directly related to the assignment; very basic vocabulary with frequent errors.

ORGANIZATION

Excellent: Clear introduction directed in an interesting way toward a specific audience; paragraph(s) developed with specific academic format: topic sentence, logical support with substantial specific data; successful use of coherence devices within sentences and between sentences; clear conclusion.

Above Average: Obvious beginning/middle/end; division of central ideas into smaller parts; awareness of audience; paragraph(s) flawed in development and/or logic; coherence within sentences and between sentences, but some choppiness; conclusion often a simple restatement.

Average:	Intent to develop central idea; some sense of beginning/middle/end; occasional wandering from topic; some development of ideas; general statements predominate; limited use of coherence devices, especially between sentences; conclusion simply stated or missing.
Fair:	Limited organization beyond the sentence level; thoughts written down as they come to mind; no introduction or conclusion; coherence limited to internal sentence connectors.
Poor:	No apparent organization; no introduction or conclusion; no focus; little or no development; no coherence devices.

In addition to a placement writing sample, you might administer a short answer test which requires the students to write under the pressure of time. A class period either before or after such a test might be spent delineating the characteristics of short answer tests and the skills needed to write them successfully. If your students have various major fields, you might go to the test center on your campus and find short answer questions there in the various major fields. Or you might use questions such as these:

A. Write a brief report about the most serious problem you encountered during your first month in the U.S. (5 minutes)
B. Describe what you consider your basic problem in writing English. Give specific examples to support your opinion. (5 minutes)
C. List three ways the structure of your native language differs from English. Give a specific example to support each point you make. (10 minutes)
D. Translate a short joke from your language into English. (10 minutes)

In addition to these forms of placement, the students should have the opportunity to write one or two paragraphs at home during the first week of class on topics which they choose. These paragraphs will give you more information and will provide samples for revision (more on revision below).

During the first week of class, assign the students a careful reading of the course objectives. Explain that classes in specific fields have specific vocabulary (terminology): genetics, agriculture, psychology, etc. The same is true in the study of composition, and the vocabulary on the first pages of the text will be used throughout the course. Discussion of these pages can be limited or expanded. You may wish to discuss the foundations of writing:

A. Writing is practical communication; conciseness and clarity are necessary in every field.

B.   Writing is an educational process in which the writer
     is solely responsible for communicating.
C.   Writing is a process of organization, analysis, and
     synthesis.
D.   Writers always write for an audience.
E.   Writers should always write about what they know
     about.

Revision

Many students have a fatalistic outlook about their writing:
"What's done is done;" "It's in Allah's hands." Many have no
concept of either the rough draft or revisions. But
recognition of errors, realization of individual writing
weaknesses, and correction are essential for better writing.
Revising means "looking again," and students who revise often
learn as much from the "looking again" as they did from writing
in the first place.

To encourage students to revise, grade the revisions (+ or -, S
or U, or letter grades). Often this takes very little time
especially after the first two weeks of class, because by then
the students realize that you mean business. With your
constant monitoring, most students will finally learn that
revision in itself is valuable.

However, most students need to be taught how to revise.
Revision differs from rewriting because the students correct
only the errors in their work. Revision, of course, can
include adding to or changing detail, changing the order or
material in paragraphs, or eliminating parts of an essay.

The first time you hand back a writing assignment, you will
probably spend most of the class period going over the process
of revision and having the students begin their revisions
during class. You will have to make available to the students
a correction symbol sheet which lists the marks you make on
their papers (a kind of shorthand) and the explanations of
those marks. You might also include suggestions for correcting
each error, as in the sample below:

   Sp   spelling error; correct the word and spell it five
           times on the back of the previous page.

   Agr   agreement problem; the subject and verb do not
           agree, or the pronoun and its referent do not
           agree; correct the error above the original.

   F   wrong form of word; you have used, for example, an
           adjective instead of an adverb; correct the error
           above the original.

For ease in grading revisions:

   A.   have the students write on one side of the page and
        revise on the back of the previous page for long
        revisions (sentences, phrases). An illustration which

may help the students follows:

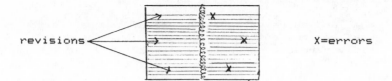

revisions   X=errors

B. have the students use a different color of ink or
   pencil to revise.
C. small errors (punctuation, verb tense) may be
   corrected immediately above the original error.
D. make certain that the students are fully aware of the
   correction symbols you have used.

Finally, grade the revisions with care, especially during the
first weeks. If a student continues to make an error, assign
remedial work in that area, either in Chapter 10 or in one of
the books suggested for use in remediation in that chapter.
Make certain the students correct every error you mark and make
the necessary changes that you have suggested; encourage them
to ask questions in the margins if they do not understand.
Then make it obvious that you noticed if the revisions were not
complete.

Inevitably, some students will balk at revisions, and some will
continue to be recalcitrant (or indifferent) throughout the
course. But those who work hard at revising will find their
writing improving, and at the end of the course they may remark
on the validity of revision. Those same students will find the
rough draft (and brainstorming and outlining) useful, and they
will learn that the final draft of an essay is the result of a
process, a combination of inspiration and perspiration.

The Audience

If this course is to be advantageous, students must realize
that no writing takes place in a vacuum, that all writing has a
purpose and an audience. Having the students choose their
topics for most of the writing done in the course is the first
step towards relevance. Another is your assistance in helping
them discover for whom they are writing--before they write.
This audience might be the teacher, or it might be the rest of
the class; perhaps a student will choose to write a paper for
an academic class, and so the audience will be a professor. In
each case, it is important that the students understand that
both the form and the content of the papers they write must
fulfill the expectations of the U.S. academic audience.

To establish a sense of audience in the class, and to teach the
processes as well as the products of writing, have the students
bring rough drafts of their paragraphs/essays to class. Divide
the students into groups of 3-4. Select the groups carefully
at first: a talkative student, a quiet student, a

knowledgeable student, a poor student. Have the students read each other's papers carefully. Then, at least the first time, lead the discussion about the drafts:

A. What do you remember about one of the papers you read?
B. What was the best part of one of the papers?
C. Did you read a paper you enjoyed? Why did you enjoy it?

After the initial comments, ask the students to talk with one another and to make one suggestion on how to make the paper better.

At first students will have difficulty (even with the handwriting!), and their comments will be, "Interesting," "I liked it," "It was good." But eventually their self-confidence and knowledge will increase, and they will feel more at ease with their peers; the students will begin to learn from one another. One of the more important lessons students can learn from reading peer papers is that if they bring a completed rough draft to class, they can be assured of getting some advice on how to make the paper better. Inevitably, this results in a better final draft. Later in the course you can ask them to look for more specific things in the drafts: topic sentences, transitions, logical fallacies, etc.

Two problems occur with small group work on rough drafts:

A. students who are absent or who come without a paper
B. students who are never really able to critique a paper

In each case, the advantages for the remaining (majority of) students are still significant, and even the students who do not participate fully in the exercise will benefit from hearing peers discuss papers. Moreover, the teacher, who circulates among the groups, reading, offering suggestions, mini-conferencing, can make the group a learning situation even for those who have no papers.

The most significant advantages of this approach:

A. suggestions from peers concerning content or grammar are often less painful than similar suggestions from the teacher
B. positive feedback from peers is great motivation
C. students from different language backgrounds will be able to correct each other's grammatical errors with relative ease

Showing and Telling

The class in which you teach showing and telling is vital to the course. It must be a class which the students will remember, a class you will refer to during the semester whenever the discussion of specific detail arises. As many as two class periods can be spent discussing and practicing the basic difference between showing and telling.

The most important fact you will teach the students is that merely asserting does not validate a statement in English academic writing; one person's opinion is worthless by itself. This is a difficult concept to teach even native-speakers; for international students, who very likely come from a culture in which the use of specific detail is considered belittling, the problem is even more significant. But the students must understand that in the writing you are preparing them to do, simply _telling_ an audience will not be of interest or value to their audience; only by supplying specific detail, by _showing_, will the material be acceptable.

You might explain that often students who regularly write very short paragraphs (or essays) are probably only _telling_. Naturally, they'll be finished in a much shorter time and space. For these students (and for most of your ESL students), practicing _showing_ can change both their writing and their attitudes toward writing. The problem of simply telling is actually much easier to solve than that of the student who is wordy and repetitious. Students who say, "I've already said everything I have to say," at the end of three sentences are usually the students who have already _told_ everything they have to tell. Adding specific detail can expand that writing and make it more interesting for the reader.

After initial comments about showing and telling, ask the students what process they follow when they write. The list might include:

A. Initial panic
B. WHAT will I write? (Students may say, "What does the teacher want?" but the question should be "What will interest my audience?")
C. Decision: a kind of _focus_
D. Notes? Outlining? Brainstorming?
E. Actual writing
F. Revision
G. Final draft

Following this discussion, read and discuss thoroughly some sample paragraphs. The "mother" paragraphs in the textbook are all poor examples of "showing" for a variety of reasons (discussed below). Be absolutely merciless with the samples (therefore, using samples of student work from your class would not be suitable), and ask the students to think about what they wrote on earlier samples as you discuss these.

Evaluation of the "mother" paragraphs (pp. 3-4)

1. Colloquial language ("Maw"), confusing first sentence (What's "it"? and who's "she"?). The paragraph is all _telling_: the reader has a right to ask the writer to _show_ such phrases as "best care," "taught me more," "overflowing with love," "always understanding," and "easy to communicate with." Each of these phrases could function as a single area of description that could then be explained and clarified and illustrated in a paragraph. Example:

the paragraph could be written entirely about how understanding the mother is (in what ways? what kinds of examples could this writer use?). This paragraph is really filled with generalizations about the genus of mother when what the audience needs is more specific information about this particular mother.

2. Just the physical description helps the audience visualize something about the mother; it makes her real. And there is memorable detail about backing up in the field that shows how difficult and determined this mother can be. But the last sentences deteriorate into generalities. The audience should want to know more about her "stories": what were they? This sentence alone could be the first sentence of another paragraph which could be illustrated. The last two sentences in the paragraph are primarily about the writer, not the mother, and they grow more general with each word. Ask the students how they might illustrate the last sentence.

3. The first sentence is "elbow-greasing;" that is, it's writing what first comes to the writer's mind. This writer starts writing and hopes to get to the point eventually. This form of "pre-writing" should be excluded from the paragraph before turning it in. The next two sentences are more about the writer than the mother, and later in the paragraph the writer brings in both siblings and father. However, the heart of the paragraph, the part about the mother going back to school, is of interest to the audience. Now the writer needs to cut all the irrelevant material: the generalities about the mother ("always there," "easy to talk to," "keeps up everything"), and more importantly, the irrelevant material about the rest of the family. The audience needs more specific material about what makes this mother unique. Show how much she loves teaching; show how she made the decision to go back to school. Ask the students to give information that could make the paragraph more memorable.

4. This paragraph does nothing but tell. Moreover, the second sentence contradicts the first (the first says the mother is capable of coping, and the second indicates that she goes to pieces easily). Neither sentence is shown. The audience should be demanding, "Show us 'most excitable.'" The last two sentences are about the author, not about the mother, and they therefore are irrelevant.

5. The language in this paragraph is fairly sophisticated, but the result sounds encyclopedic. It fulfills the letter of the assignment but is not very memorable or interesting to the audience. The objectivity in this sample will be necessary in most of the forms of university writing the students will do in this course, but it is not particularly desirable in a paragraph which is supposed to describe a unique mother to an audience of peers.

You might point out to the students that these writers might have been more successful if they had followed a process before beginning to write:

    A.   Questions (pre-writing):
          1.   What makes my mother different from everyone else's mother?
          2.   What can I tell my audience about my mother that will make that audience willing to read the paragraph?
          3.   What information can I give to show that my telling sentence(s) are valid, interesting, valuable, and memorable?

    B.   Selection
          1.   Focus on a single aspect of the mother (a slice of the "mother pie")
             (a)   consider what is known (specific details)
             (b)   consider the audience
          2.   Make notes: select the best details

    C.   Articulation
          1.   Write the paragraph (rough draft)
          2.   Revise that paragraph
          3.   Write the final draft of that paragraph

The students will probably be momentarily terrified of your expectations by the time you finish evaluating the sample paragraphs, but some will be able to criticize and offer specific details even as you proceed through the paragraphs, and everyone will remember the lesson of using specific detail. In addition, you will be laying the groundwork for further discussion on writing for an audience, on topic focus, on unity and completeness in paragraphs, and on topic sentences.

The following day, you might ask students what they wrote about; then have the other students in class ask questions about the topic which they might expect the author to answer in the paragraphs. You may in addition want to ditto some of your students' samples now that they have had a chance to write a paragraph at home, especially if you feel that the students need more work in showing and telling. Or you may want to ditto some more successful mother paragraphs which you and the class can discuss. Two samples follow: the first, although it is written in first person and seems to deal with the experiences of the writer, is actually about the mother, and it is a good example of a paragraph with specific detail which is memorable. Ask the students to look away after reading the text, and then ask them what they remember, or have them read the paragraphs at home and ask them the following day what they remember. In the second paragraph, the humor makes the non-typical mother interesting to the audience, and all the details are directly related to the first sentence.

    When I left home to go to college, I missed my mother. I missed her coming into the house after work, changing from her uniform into a housedress and comfortable slippers, and starting dinner. I missed her salt and pepper hair, the smell of her cigarette smoke, and her matter-of-fact

way of dealing with problems.   As the weeks of school
passed, the emptiness of not having her warmth and
generosity and good advice began to fade.   But one day
near Thanksgiving, my roommate and I went to a nearby
hospital to visit some elderly, bed-ridden patients.   As I
walked into the hospital, a wave of homesickness washed
over me, and tears came to my eyes.   For a moment, I
couldn't understand why I missed my mother so suddenly;
then I realized that the smell of the hospital was part of
my mother.   When she came home from her job as an
emergency room nurse, her uniform held the smell of the
hospital, and although I had never thought about it
before, the hospital smell was an intimate part of my
life.

My mother is a loving person, like most mothers, but
unlike most mothers, she is a terrible cook.   Canned foods
and MacDonald's hamburgers are her salvation; heating up
canned spaghetti or driving down to the big golden arches
is her style for dinner.   If she has to cook, the result
is often disaster; in fact, the napkin is usually the best
part of the meal.   Burned chicken, gooey rice, sodden
beans, and charred rolls are standard, and sometimes the
meal is even more spectacular: a cheese casserole that
won't come out of the pan, turnip soup which is inedible,
or pork chops that catch fire in the oven.   My mother
cooks only on rare occasions, and for that her family is
grateful.

Another way of showing the student that good paragraphs must
include specific detail is to work through the page of
paragraphs which were written by students about their names (p.
5).   Students can easily spot which specific details make those
paragraphs memorable.

General and Specific

Being able to distinguish levels of generality is necessary for
any student.   Students who lack this skill will continue to
have difficulty in using specific detail to support general
statements.   The problem will be compounded when these students
begin to outline essays; the exercises in the textbook on
general and specific (pp. 6-7) are precursors of the outlining
(subheading) process that demonstrates the expectations of the
academic audience.   Discover whether or not your students
understand the concept of general/specific, and spend the time
necessary for adequate comprehension.

Basic Organization

Review paragraph structure with the students: indenting, the
validity of using a topic sentence, the fact that a paragraph
is about one (main) idea.   The topic sentence tells what the
paragraph is about while the remaining sentences explain,
describe, and illustrate (i.e., show) the topic sentence.
Stress the fact that the straightforward presentation will

increase communication with a U.S. academic audience because
this audience will more easily understand the way in which
material is presented. Paragraph topics for this week may be
chosen by the students, or you might suggest possibilities,
such as those below, which will give the students practice in
basic forms of organization:
  A. How I Found My Apartment
  B. What I Do When I Am Sick
  C. Describe what a stranger would see if you showed him a
      photograph of your family.

Subject and Topic

Between thought and articulation comes selection; without pre-
writing and selection, articulation will be poor. Students may
say that they have nothing to write about, but in fact, they
have so many things to write about that selection, not
articulation, is the problem. Rarely does a student narrow a
topic too far; the tendency is, "If I choose a big enough
topic, I'll certainly have enough to tell." That, of course,
is the problem. If a student's topic is too broad, he will
never get beyond the telling stage, will never get to the
specifics (showing) so necessary in successful academic
writing.

While discussing Exercise 10, stress pre-writing and narrowing.
Ask several students to put their topics on the board, and then
work with them, indicating which topics would be viable
paragraph/essay/book topics. Have other students indicate what
questions they could ask about each topic and what information
they would expect to find in the paragraph that followed.

Example: Camping (a broad subject, not yet narrowed to a
          topic)

  A. What could the student write about camping?
  B. Who is the audience? (Is the paragraph directed
      toward beginners? Is the writer trying to convince
      his audience to try camping? Is the information for
      experts in camping?)
  C. What must the writer tell the audience about camping?
      What specific details should the paragraph contain?
  D. What is the purpose of the paragraph?

In a very broad topic like the one above, the students will
gave a variety of suggestions and will eventually see that the
topic is a subject and as such has no focus. The writer must
therefore narrow the subject to a topic, probably using the
following process:

  A. identification of audience:_____
  B. what the writer wants to communicate about camping to
      that audience:_____
  C. what specific details the writer can use to show what
      he wants to tell:_____

Once the students have learned to narrow subjects to topics,

the organization of material will be significantly simplified.
But working with several student-selected topics on the board,
the entire class benefits.

Topic Sentences

For many students, the initial discussion of topic sentences
will be review. In class, work with student topics after
discussing the basic tenets of the topic sentence.   Have
students write topic sentences on the board and circle the
controlling ideas. Have other students "fill in" what they
expect in the rest of the paragraph. Stress the concepts of
controlling ideas and of the difference between a statement of
opinion and a statement of intent. Paragraph assignments for
this section should come from the lists of topics the students
have made; these lists may continue to grow, and students
should be encouraged to add to them. Indeed, the student-
selected topics may be used twice: once for a paragraph, and
later for expansion into or inclusion in an essay on the same
topic.

Below are the solutions to the exercises on the topic sentence
(pp. 12-13). All of the sentences use are student samples.
For additional exercises, use the topic sentences of students
in the class from the past week.

EXERCISE 1E

Circle the controlling ideas and write questions concerning
each topic sentence.

1. There are (differences) in (shape,) (color,) and (taste) between
    the (two) most (popular varieties of dates in Saudi Arabia.)
    Questions: what differences? what are the effects of the
                differences? what are the two varieties?

2. One of the most (recent technical advances) in man's (use of
    water) is the (development of hydroelectric power.)
    Questions: what is hydroelectric power? how has it
                advanced technology? how recent is the
                development?

3. The (creativity) of the (pre-school child) can be (developed)
    with special (activities.)
    Questions: what special activities? how are they used?
                what is their effect on the creativity of young
                children?

4. (Violence) in the sport of (hockey) is (destroying) the (quality)
    of the game.
    Questions: what kind of violence? how is it destructive?
                how is the quality being destroyed?

The Point Paragraph

The "point paragraph" is not only a reinforcement of the

concepts of general and specific; it is also an introduction to the heading/supporting detail organization common in U.S. academic prose. It is not outlining as <u>pre-writing</u> but rather a way of patterning material that the students have generated in a format that will fulfill the expectations of the U.S. academic audience.

Exercise 1G gives the students an opportunity to produce a point outline. Working with student topics on the board is also helpful, and having students construct outlines in small groups or in pairs also works well. Assigning the "planning of a paragraph" rather than the paragraph itself provides additional practice for the students, and having the students write a paragraph from an outline for another assignment reinforces the value of the point outline. For example, students might write outlines on Monday and Wednesday, and the accompanying paragraphs on Tuesday and Thursday for homework, or students might make an outline for homework, then write the paragraph in class the following day.

The Process of Writing a Paragraph

This review, on pages 14-15, can become a touchstone for all further writing, and students will be referred to the Revision Guidelines on page 16 throughout the next few chapters.

CHAPTER 2: DEVELOPING AND SUPPORTING IDEAS

This chapter has been specifically divided and classified to help the students with basic academic writing skills. First, different planning strategies are illustrated, along with the resulting paragraphs. Students should discuss their various pre-writing/planning strategies. A lecture on right/left brain, perceptual learning styles, or the like can provide a good introduction to the main objective of this chapter: to persuade students that different students prepare to write in different ways; that brainstorming and outlining might be thought of as opposite ends of a continuum with flow charts, trees, and bubbles somewhere along the continuum. Many students have a variety of coping skills, while a few use only a single strategy regardless of the assignment, the audience, and the available material. Students in this class should have the opportunity to experiment with several pre-writing strategies, discovering which suits them best in diverse writing situations.

Techniques of Support

Having learned that each paragraph has a particular structure--a topic sentence followed by 4-8 sentences of support--the students must now learn how to support the topic sentence. The techniques presented here are those generally used in most academic paragraphs to support a topic sentence, and the students should understand that these "supporters" will be used in every paragraph they write during the remainder of this course (and most probably in any academic writing they will do later).

Sample paragraphs in this section demonstrate the use of each technique; writing assignments should emphasize the use of one or more of the supporting techniques. Eventually, students will need to understand that more than one technique of support can be used in a single paragraph, that indeed the techniques often overlap. However, just as in the science lab, analysis (taking apart and observing) precedes synthesis (putting back together).

Students may choose topics from their own lists, or you may suggest a single topic which is then worked into 4 different topic sentences, each supported by a different technique:

Example: Swimming (to be narrowed to 4 different topic
          sentences)

    A.   How to Do the Backstroke (facts)
    B.   Kinds of Nine-Year-Old Swimmers (physical description)
    C.   Why Swimming is Good Exercise (examples)
    D.   A Nearly Fatal Swimming Accident (personal experience)

Student topics on the board could provide additional work. Have other students in the class answer these questions about the board topics:

A. What could the topic sentence be for this topic?
B. What are the controlling ideas in this topic sentence?
C. What question(s) could the writer ask about that topic sentence?
D. What technique(s) of support could be used to make the topic sentence interesting and valuable to the audience?

NOTE: During the section about physical description, you may want to spend additional time discussing denotation and connotation. It is helpful to bring a thesaurus to class, and you might even encourage some of the students to investigate different kinds of thesauruses: remind them that Roget's Thesaurus is sometimes divided by category rather than alphabetically; the former is much more difficult to use. The new Webster's Thesaurus is very expensive, but students who intend to study language when they finish the course may need its thoroughness in presentation and usage.

In addition to the thesaurus, you might want to discuss regular dictionaries; again, bringing several to class for investigation is helpful. Students need to understand that there is no perfect dictionary, and that they should choose one which fits their needs. The American Heritage Dictionary, for example, is much more colloquial in its selection than many Webster's editions (but Webster's name was not copyrighted, so many dictionaries bear his name). For a newly revised (rather than simply reprinted) dictionary, students can check for words which have only recently come into the language: android, bionic, superconductor, fast food, etc.

Methods of Development

This section is a fairly traditional presentation of ways to develop a paragraph. The distinction between techniques of support (supporters) and methods of development needs to be explained to the students. The writer chooses a method of development which will best present his/her material to the reader; s/he then chooses supporters which will best prove (support, explain, illustrate) the topic sentence. Assignments in this section ask students to label both supporters and the method(s) of development in each paragraph.

Process

You may wish to spend part of a period studying passive voice (Chapter 10) because passive voice is such a common element of most scientific process writing. Science and technology majors should understand that passive voice is widely used in their textbooks and journals in the interest of objective reporting. In addition, you should stress the various techniques of support available to students writing process paragraphs: facts, examples, etc.

Definition/Extended Definition

Extended definition is probably the best place to differentiate
techniques of support from methods of development. In this
week's paragraphs, and in future expository essays and research
papers, this method of development will often be used. It is
not unusual to see all four supporters in an extended
definition paragraph. Stress the problems in choosing abstract
topics for paragraphs as you teach the exercises on pages 34-
35; abstractions are difficult to explain (i.e., define)
accurately and specifically.

Comparison/Contrast

Work with a student-selected topic on the board; try to
organize it in both of the ways explained in the book:

Example: Married life vs. single life

FORM #1	FORM #2
Married life 1. 2.　advantages and 3.　　disadvantages	Married life and single life 1. 2.　　　advantages 3.
Single life 1. 2.　advantages and 3.　　disadvantages	Married life and single life 1. 2.　　disadvantages 3.

The process of writing a comparison/contrast paragraph follows
the process for other paragraphs, but there are two additional
pre-writing steps:

    A.   making a list (like the one above)
    B.   choosing a side
           THEN
    C.   constructing a topic sentence, etc.

Discuss purpose: why would a writer employ comparison/contrast
as a method of development? To explain? to persuade that X is
easier/better than Y?

Classification

Classification looks easy, but accurate classification is
difficult in practice. However, it is a necessary skill for
academic writing. Teaching classification is also an
opportunity for additional work on levels of specificity. Be
certain that the students can produce valid, parallel
classifications. It may be helpful to work with parallelism
(Chapter 10) before tackling the parallelism in thought that is
necessary for classification.

Work with various classification exercises on the board:

Examples:

Pilots		Party-Goers	
A. fat		A. drunks	
B. thin	(overlapping	B. sex fiends	(inadequate
C. tall	classes)	C. the good guys	division of
D. short			classes)
(Can't a pilot be both		(Is everyone but the	
tall and fat?)		writer evil?)	

Use student classification of the exercise topics as well; they
will often contain flaws in classification, and the students
themselves will begin to correct them.

Cause-Effect

Because cause-effect paragraphs are the first step toward
argumentative (or problem-solving or persuasive) essays,
students must understand this method of development thoroughly.
Make certain that the students fully comprehend the difference
between a cause and an effect, the fact that time is involved
in any discussion of cause-effect, and that effects can become
causes and causes can become effects in a chain of events. The
problems of time and cause-effect can be illustrated:

> A DC-10 which crashed in Chicago was initially reported to
> have crashed as a result of a broken wing-bolt. The bolt
> was reported to be the cause of the engine falling off
> (thus causing the crash). Later investigation showed that
> when the wing fell off, the bolt broke. Therefore, the
> broken bolt was an effect, not the cause, of the crash.

Have the students work in small groups or in pairs with
Exercises 2L and 2M. Small groups/pairs could also construct
topic sentences on the board; then have class members decide
what supporters would result in a good paragraph.

You might choose to review cause-effect sentence connectors:
because, so, therefore, consequently. Their appropriate use in
terms of time (what happened first, what resulted) can be shown
in a board reproduction of the chart below. The use of
punctuation in the use of these connectors can be taught from
the section in Chapter 10 which deals with sentence structure:
semi-colons, commas, colons.

19

Cause-Effect Connectors (X = cause, Y = effect)	
short word (coordinating conjunction)	X, so Y
long words (conjunctive adverbs)	X; therefore, Y X; consequently, Y X; as a result, Y
subordinating words: notice that in the use of because, the cause occurs immediately after because	Y because X Because X, Y

The spiralling effect of the textbook begins here; the skills taught in the paragraph section are re-introduced and reinforced. Students should read and discuss in class the general introduction to the essay. The first assigned essay might be done piecemeal: selection of topic, thesis + topic sentences, point outline of 3 body paragraphs, rough draft, final draft. By completing pieces of the essay on a succession of nights, students will learn that an essay is indeed made up of parts, and that they have time to consider a variety of supporters and developers. Revision is also easier: paragraphs are shorter and initially more manageable to revise than an entire essay. In addition, the writing of an essay in parts helps the students see that an essay can be constructed much as a picture puzzle is put together: piece by piece, trying first one piece and then another, shifting pieces around until everything fits.

Peer Evaluation

Students should spend parts of several class periods helping each other, being audience as well as author. Guided peer evaluation is probably more successful than just letting students "at" each other. Perhaps starting with the student essay at the end of the chapter would offer the students good, non-personal practice. Then, as students read each other's essays, write, and then discuss, you could circle the class, mini-conferencing, moderating, stimulating. You are an integral part of this process, and the students should look to you for leadership, especially in the early stages of the peer evaluation processes.

Begin by discussing possible topics. Stress again that:

A. students may select their own topics, perhaps one of the topics they have already written a paragraph about. Some students may need to revise or add to their list of topics.
B. qualifying and specifying topics will make the essay easier to write. Working with student topics on the board and encouraging all the students to help with the organization of these topics will enhance the learning process:
    1. What could a suitable thesis for this topic be?
    2. What are the controlling ideas in this thesis?
    3. What material could be used with this topic?
    4. What techniques of support? methods of development?

The overall organization of an essay (introduction, body, conclusion) is explained in some detail in the textbook, and much of the information will be familiar to the students. Board work with student samples is vital; exercises might include:

A. After the topic has been suitably narrowed, have the
    students write a single body paragraph first.
    Starting in the middle of the essay may not be
    absolutely logical, but since the students have been
    writing "body paragraphs" during the first weeks of
    the course, this assignment should not be difficult.
    The following day, have two or three students write
    their body paragraph topic sentences on the board.
    Have other class members "fill in" what they expect in
    the paragraph.

B. Have small groups of students work together to write a
    body paragraph for a topic sentence which you (or
    they) supply. Have the groups exchange paragraphs;
    have them read and discuss the exchanged paragraphs.

C. Have the students write individual introductions for
    homework. Ask some students to write their theses on
    the board the following day. Have the rest of the
    class suggest what should/could/might come before each
    thesis, i.e., the introductory material. Perhaps they
    might also suggest what might follow the thesis:
    topic sentence, paragraph organization, etc.

D. Have the students read each other's work (the rough
    draft). Have them correct any grammar errors, ask
    questions of the writer to improve the content, make
    suggestions for more support, etc. Or have the
    students read each other's final draft, then indicate
    the strengths of the essay: what was interesting,
    valuable, or memorable, and why. Peer in-put and
    evaluation such as this are helpful for teacher and
    student alike.

Have the students turn in their rough drafts as well as their
final drafts. In this way you can see how they revised and
that they revised.

The Thesis Statement

The easiest way to teach the thesis statement is to stress the
parallel functions of the thesis and the topic sentence. Just
as the topic sentence is the most general and most important
sentence in a paragraph, the thesis is the most general and
most important statement in the essay. And the thesis is
integrally linked to the topic sentences in an essay. From the
controlling ideas in the thesis come the topic sentences for
the body paragraphs.

Work with the exercises concerning the thesis statement and its
relationship with the topic sentences in class (pp. 52-55).
Additional examples can come from student samples or from
exercises such as the one below:

Example: Using the following thesis statements, construct
          topic sentences for the body paragraphs that could
          follow each thesis.

1. Teenage marriages have several disadvantages.
2. The Libyan government has recently developed and improved health facilities in three areas: medical training, hospitals, and health education of the populace.
3. A successful choir depends on the age, the self-discipline, and the dedication of its members.
4. Religion played an important part in my life.
5. In Thailand, the people have three different ways to grow crops, depending on their incomes.
6. Cooking can be a rewarding experience.
7. Solar energy has great potential for use in Saudi Arabia.
8. Spending a vacation in Plata, a fishing port in Argentina, is a pleasant experience.

Questions:

1. Circle the controlling ideas in each thesis statement and in all of the topic sentences you construct.
2. Which thesis statement above is a statement of opinion? A statement of intent?
3. What methods of development could be used in the body paragraphs of each essay? Which techniques of support?

Introductions and Conclusions

The information on introductions and conclusions is very narrowly presented. Of course, there are many other ways to write both the introduction and the conclusion. But the steps given in the text, and the suggestions for writing introductions and conclusions, will be especially helpful for students who have never done much writing even in their native languages. If these students can gain a perception of how introductions are structured, their papers will immediately begin and end more successfully. The surprising thing about teaching the writing process is that so few of the students actually know what makes successful writing even in their native languages, much less what constitutes successful writing in U.S. academic prose.

Answers to Exercises

Exercise 3J

1. (Watershed management) has not progressed because there are three major problems: the invasion of watershed areas by the populace, the lack of research by the scientists, and the deficiencies of budget and personnel of the government in Thailand.
2. the three problems mentioned in the thesis
3. solution
4. major field professor? colleagues in the field? the Thai government?

Exercise 3K

1. The importance of the TOEFL for the audience (i.e.,
   other international students)
2. primarily examples and personal experience although
   the other two will also be used
3. yes
4. solutions

Exercise 3L

1. opinion (better); intent, also
2. progress; graduate students; better than
   undergraduates
3. cause-effect; comparison/contrast
4. Why do graduate students make better progress? What
   prevents undergraduates from making progress? In what
   ways do the "needs" of graduates and undergraduates
   differ?

NOTE: typing a ditto with just your students' introductions
       and conclusions (from the rough drafts, if possible) is
       an excellent way of teaching introductions, conclusions,
       overall organization, use of questions about topic
       sentences, and use of specific detail.

CHAPTER 4: DRAFTING AND REVISING THE ESSAY

Students will write a second expository essay as you work
through this chapter. The process they will use will be
similar to the one used in the previous week: selection of
topic, narrowing, pre-writing, construction of thesis statement
and topic sentences, decisions about methods of development and
techniques of support. In addition, students will concentrate
on the drafting and revising processes so necessary in
successful writing, and they will learn more about coherence
devices, particularly transitional words and phrases. Again,
board work (or, perhaps, student conferences, or both) will
help the students understand the articulation of the
assignment. In-class work on composing, peer evaluation, and
small group work are efficient and successful ways to teach
students the complete essay.

Coherence Devices

Because transitional words and phrases are often relatively
meaningless (although they have very specific functions within
a sentence of a paragraph), and because other inner paragraph
coherence devices (i.e., the use of pronouns, repetition of
key words and phrases) are used without conscious decision in
most speech, teaching coherence devices can be frustrating.
For the students, experimenting with awkward-sounding
transitions and repeating key words (which, not incidentally,
would not be necessary in their native languages) may seem
strange and quite childish; the transitions seem to stick out
on their papers like warts on a finger. But these words are
absolutely essential to successful writing, so the students
must learn to use them correctly. Perhaps showing them how
transitions and connectors work in actual prose (Time Magazine,
journals from major fields) will reinforce the lesson.

The transitions in the textbook are listed according to classes
and according to structure (i.e., subordinating words,
coordinating words, etc.). These classes not only provide a
basis for usage but can also be used to review methods of
development, techniques of support, and the sentence structure
exercises in Chapter 10. Note that specific paragraphs or
essays in which the coherence devices have been used are
indicated for each class of transitions. Use these specific
examples as you go through the list with the students. Be
certain to point out that this list is not complete; it is just
a beginning. Many more transitional words and phrases exist;
this list is comprised of some of the most common transitions.
In the past, students in this course have found that this list
continues to be helpful after the class has ended. Some have
taped these pages to bulletin boards for future use in their
academic work.

Paragraph hooks are satisfying to teach. Often the concept is
entirely new to the students; coherence between paragraphs may
never have occurred to them. But the simplicity of the use of
the paragraph hook makes it easy to learn, easy to apply, and

almost always immediately successful. The student's writing
seems better immediately.

NOTE: It is possible to teach these coherence devices earlier
        in the course; however, the improvement in student
        writing is so evident when coherence devices are used
        that the students should learn the basic rules for
        coherence first: clear thought, careful organization
        (both overall and inner-paragraph), and selection of
        relevant material. The use of coherence devices adds
        coherence, but it does not impose coherence on an
        otherwise unorganized paragraph/essay.

Exercise 4B

Underline the transitions in the passages below. Underline
with wavy lines the repetition of key words and phrases. Put
pronouns that function as coherence devices in parentheses.

                              #1

One way that (K-Mart) makes so much (money) is with the famous
flashing (blue light) Drawing shoppers like flies to garbage
cans, the famous "blue-light specials" unload all types of
slow-moving merchandise. Whether it is sandals in a snowstorm,
Halloween costumes in November, or day-old ham and cheese
sandwiches, the blue light disposes of this merchandise which
thrifty shoppers devour like hungry dogs. Because (they) are
caught up in the excitement and spirit of the moment, many
shoppers take advantage of these specials to buy that new
screwdriver that (they) may never use or that blouse that
doesn't quite fit. In addition, by purchasing the cheapest,
most poorly constructed items, these shoppers assure K-Mart
that (they) will return in a month to buy replacements. The
blue-light specials are one sure way that K-Mart extracts $100
annually from every square foot of selling space in (its)
stores.

26

If the (University of Spain) decided to use a ("selective system")
as a base for (its) (enrollment,) both the (students) and the
(university) would (benefit.) Under the present open enrollment
policy, anyone who chooses can begin university work;
consequently, many students leave (their) studies after two or
three years, and only a few students finish (their) degrees.
For example, in the most popular fields, like medicine and
engineering, thousands of students begin each year, yet only
25% complete (their) work. As a result, the students become
frustrated because (they) have to spend additional time finding
another field to study or finding a job. The university also
suffers because education costs money, and the money used for
these students is lost when (they) do not finish. A selective
examination would distinguish between students who have the
aptitude and the desire to do university work and (those) who
do not.

Revision

During the week, emphasize the lessons of the previous week's
essay; this reinforcement may come when you return last week's
essays and may begin the revising process. Students should
gain confidence in completing the final draft of this week's
essays as they revise the essay from the previous week.

Research on composing and revising strategies with both native
and non-native speakers of English shows that writers differ in
their approaches. For some writers, revision processes occur
as an integral part of the composing processes: to write, then
revise, rewrite, then revise. Mature, experienced writers are
capable of major changes (e.g., re-ordering sentences and
paragraphs, adding or eliminating material, rewriting the
introduction) while less experienced, developmental writers
often make only small, corrective, editing changes (e.g.,
spelling, combining two sentences).

For some, those who are "back-burners" (i.e., they do most of
their composing internally, then write relatively finished
drafts), revision is little more than editing; for others

(i.e., brainstormers who compose in stream-of-consciousness style), selecting and revising material is a major part of their writing processes, through which they often "discover" what they choose to communicate.

Students who are developing writers rarely have revision skills. Yet writing teachers know the value of such skills. Therefore, you must be able to take the time--class time--to provide the students with the necessary "schema" to do adequate revisions.

The section on revision in this chapter provides guidelines that will help the students focus on their writing from a variety of perspectives. However, they will still need considerable teacher support and positive feedback.

Peer revision, of course, is another way for writers to receive input about their writing. Using the Peer Revision Checklist, first with the student essays at the end of the chapter, and then with essays from your students, will add to the students' confidence.

As you continue through this chapter, students may need the practice of writing another expository essay. As they select, plan, compose, revise, and articulate this essay, you will teach coherence devices and review the processes of writing an essay. Use the sample student essays at the end of the chapter.

Or you may choose to have them write a longer essay (about 1,200 words) that is approximately double their previous essays in length. They may either choose a new topic, or they may expand one of the previous two expository essays they have written in previous weeks. This expansion can be very profitable for the students; it can show them how to add material to the points they have already made by adding a paragraph (or three), by adding specific detail to the paragraphs they already have, by revising the thesis statement to accommodate the new material, and by working through the original (now marked and revised) papers as they expand them.

Other possible topics for this week's assignment:

A. a cause-effect expository essay (700-900 words)
B. an expository essay which examines a topic the student may want to use in the research paper (the research paper will then be an expansion of this essay)

Whichever assignment the students do, as a mid-term check on what the students have learned, you might ask them to do the following:

A. make notes; then construct an outline
B. write a rough draft and then make appropriate revisions
C. turn in all notes, the outline, and the rough draft

And within the final draft, have them follow these "special

instructions":

    A.   underline the thesis and the topic sentences

    B.   label the introduction and conclusion techniques (in the margin)

    C.   label the techniques of support used in three of the body paragraphs (in the margin)

    D.   label the method(s) of development used in three body paragraphs (in the margin)

    E.   circle and join the paragraph hook(s) between two body paragraphs

    F.   underline with wavy lines the transitions in one body paragraph

    G.   at the end of the essay, include the following information:

        1.   the number of words of the essay

        2.   the intended audience

        3.   the reason for writing this particular essay for this particular audience

        4.   the basic organization of the overall essay: chronological, spatial, or most important to least important point

CHAPTER 5:   PERSUASION AND THE ARGUMENTATION ESSAY

The argumentative essay seeks to persuade the reader, to convince the reader that the opinions of the writer are valid and worthwhile, perhaps to move the audience to a change of mind or even to action. The exercises in this chapter culminate in an argumentative/persuasive essay of 700-900 words.

The students need to be reminded before they start planning their argumentative essays that the basic rules of previous essay planning and writing also apply to this one:

A. write about what you know about (especially important when the writer has to persuade an audience)
B. identify the audience: perhaps the safest way to write a successful argumentative essay is to direct the essay toward an imaginary crotchety old man who is determined to disagree with everything he reads. This nasty man may be of any audience level: a major professor, a peer, a relative, etc. But whomever he represents, he is a hostile audience. Incidentally, referring to him (having him sit in the back of the classroom) during the teaching of this essay is helpful.
C. clear organization (both overall and inner paragraph) will aid in the persuasiveness of the essay
D. specific examples and solid detail to validate and strengthen the opinions in the essay are essential

In addition, the format for the argumentative essay is similar to expository prose: the introduction (background information plus thesis statement--which is always a statement of opinion in argumentation), the topic sentences at the beginning of each body paragraph which are followed by support for the controlling ideas in each topic sentence, and a conclusion.

Notice, however, that there are alternative organization forms for the body of the argumentative/persuasive essay. As you begin to work with student topics on the board, show students the options they have by spending part of each class with "live" topics. For example, on the first day, you might deal with 3-4 student topics and discuss just the viability of the topics (questions to be asked, expectations of the audience, purpose of the essay); the following day, use 3-4 more student topics, concentrating on listing pro's and con's (divide the class in half and do a mini-debate); on the next day, use 3-4 new student topics, then have the class suggest possible forms of organization for each topic. In this way, students can get help for their topics incrementally and will begin to apply lessons from other topics to their writing processes.

Board work with student topics (lists of pro's and con's, although/because statements, thesis statements and topic sentences) will help the students' writing. Look carefully for several problems that student topics may have:
    1. no controversy

2. too broad a topic
3. presenting both sides of the topic equally
    (expository, not argumentative)
4. topic is not known to the student

Having the students bring their rough drafts to class for
writing workshops (evaluation of peer papers in small groups)
will give the students a chance to identify logical fallacies
and other weaknesses in the arguments of peer papers.

Suggested process for peer evaluation of argumentative rough
drafts:
A. read the essay
B. circle any errors
C. indicate any logical fallacies in the margin
D. speak to the group; supply the following information:
    1. author and topic of the paper
    2. thesis: the side the author took
    3. form followed in the body paragraphs:
        (a) pro, pro, pro, con (pppc)
        (b) c, p, p, p
        (c) c/p, c/p, c/p, c/p
    4. technique(s) of support used
    5. the essay was/was not persuasive because...

Exercise 5F

This student sample is a classic example of an underdeveloped
argumentative/persuasive essay. Lines for support have been
added to what the student handed in. Work through the essay
(good introduction, clear thesis, clear topic sentences, solid
conclusion). Show the students how the topic sentences are not
supported, and ask for possible supporting material:
    1. Facts or Personal Experience: body paragraph #1--
        perhaps in another country, this situation actually
        occurred. Or perhaps the student could quote a
        Communist authority. Or perhaps the student has had a
        similar experience in Venezuela.
    2. Examples: body paragraph #2--Corazon Aquino and the
        Philippines seem a good example with lots of possible
        detail.
    3. Physical Description/Facts: body paragraph #3--how
        poor is El Salvador? a description of housing, or
        hungry children? or perhaps some statistics (facts)?
        What has been destroyed? Describe.
Note that the final body paragraph is not very good; the point
is obvious, and the persuasive value small. Since the student
has added so much supporting detail, s/he doesn't need this
paragraph.

NOTE: which form of organization the student chooses and
       whether or not the optional background paragraph is used
       depends upon the length of the assignment, the topic,
       the available material, and the audience (and how much
       they know). As students put their topics on the board,
       ask them which form of organization they will use. It
       won't take long to differentiate which students have one

31

very strong counter-argument, which have a couple, and
which have several counter-arguments; in the last case,
the third form of organization will probably be most
effective, especially if that student has several strong
counter-arguments. Working with the student sample
plans in Exercise 5E will help the students to choose.

An additional exercise for review that you can do with Exercise
5E:

Questions:
1. What form of overall organization will this
argumentative essay follow?
2. Circle the controlling ideas in the thesis and topic
sentences.
3. What introductory techniques are used? Concluding
technique(s)?

Logic

This section is not intended to be a complete logic course;
rather, it identifies and gives students a chance to learn
about the most common logical fallacies in student writing.
Memorizing the names of the various fallacies presented is not
necessary or even very worthwhile, but learning to identify
these fallacies in their writing will help prevent the students
from using at least the most glaring generalizations and
oversimplifications. Moreover, such practice in identifying
logic flaws will help the students to become better critical
readers as well as critical writers.

To these ends, go over the fallacies in class; from previous
course work in cause-effect paragraphs and the response to
written material, the students should already be familiar with
hasty generalization, post hoc, and ad hominum, even though
they have not encountered the formal names. Working with the
exercises in small groups before discussing the fallacy
exercises is usually fun and rewarding for both the students
and the teacher. Included below are the completed exercises;
students may have a variety of answers, and in some cases,
while their answers may not be included on the following pages,
their answers may indeed be logical.

Exercise 5H

Identify the logical fallacies below. Some sentences may have
more than one fallacy.

1. oversimplification, red herring
2. post hoc
3. oversimplification: either/or
4. stereotyping: hasty generalization
5. hasty generalization, false statistics
6. ad hominum
7. hasty generalization and oversimplification, false
statistics
8. hasty generalization

9. hasty generalization--a stereotype
10. oversimplification

Exercise 5I

Analyze the following passage in terms of logical fallacies.

Seven months ago I was in South Vietnam under the auspices of The National Education Association for the Advancement of Underdeveloped Countries. Before arriving in South Vietnam, I had studied at length the causes of political upheaval of impoverished countries and had concluded that the Buddhists were responsible for the situation in Vietnam because they refused to adjust their policies to the changing political factions.

Authority: who is the author? What is NEAAUC? Who finances it?

How long?

Concluding before he arrives?

Oversimplification
* What should he explain in the essay?

Thus, when I arrived in South Vietnam and saw a Buddhist monk engulfed in flames, my opinion was confirmed: the Buddhists want to rule South Vietnam just as the U.S. tried, before the first world war, to maintain their political and economic isolationism while secretly trying to control the British government of Lloyd George. Therefore, the single question that must be asked is, "Should the U.S. forces in Vietnam eliminate the Buddhist faction in order to effect national unity?" The answer is obvious: everything else has failed; this is the only recourse.

Concluding again

Hasty generalization

Red herring

Oversimplification

Vice and virtue words

Suspicious word
Hasty generalization; oversimplification

33

Although this may seem a startling con-   Indeed!

clusion, the facts show that only after the   Post hoc

Buddhists began to burn themselves did the

government of President Ky begin to crumble.

Indeed, should the U.S. continue to subvert   Vice and

the ideals and principles of the South Viet-   virtue words

namese when the Buddhists are the source of

the difficulty? Since Christianity teaches us

that suicide is against the laws of God, we   Red herring:
     (difference
can see that the Buddhists' political actions   between moral
     values)
are without moral justification.

Therefore, the U.S. policy-makers should

embark on a new course of action: minimize

the efforts against the Viet Cong and devote

their main force to a correction of this poi-

sonous thorn in the side of the American   Vice and
     virtue words
lamb, a thorn which is dispersing and

submersing the democratic way of life!

When you finish doing this exercise in class, it will probably
be necessary to explain to them that this is an exercise, not a
real essay at all. The cited source at the end of the essay is
fictitious. However, you might want to point out the salient
features of that citation; the students are only a week away
from beginning the research paper, and they will soon be made
aware of the fine points of citation.

Sample Student Essays

The student essays at the end of this chapter may be used in
the same way you used the essays at the end of the last
chapter: review, reinforcement, remediation for individual
students.

CHAPTER 6.   SUMMARY AND ANALYSIS

For students who already know how to write summaries, the first
part of this chapter may be unnecessary, and for those who do
not, you may need to add more practice in the skill.   Competent
summarizing is a skill, one in which all academic students need
proficiency.   If your students are summarizing in their reading
class, you may be able to integrate both classes.

To teach summary:
- A.   Students should read the article to be summarized at
least twice, first to get the "general idea(s)," and
secondly to underline or take notes on those ideas.
Identifying the controlling ideas in the thesis and
topic sentences should be relatively easy for these
students, and this exercise will reinforce what you
have been teaching.
- B.   Once the major ideas have been noted, putting them
into clear, concise sentences takes practice.   Using
some of the diction in the original article is
perfectly permissible so long as the writer uses
quotation marks and maintains the rules for accuracy
and balance.   If the students have never learned about
the rules for quotation marks, you might go over them
briefly now; the students will work with the rules of
citation again when they do their research papers.
- C.   Exercise 6A should show the student that while a
simple (10-25 word) statement of the major idea of an
article (or movie, or book, or television program, or
master's thesis, or lecture) is easy, expanding that
summary (to 50 and then to 100 words) requires
perceptive selection with, perhaps, some adjustments
in the presentation of the material.   Attaining
balance, accuracy, and conciseness is more difficult
in longer summaries.
- D.   You may want to write a summary on the board with a
topic of your own as the students are doing their
summaries (try to choose a movie or recent television
program that some of the students may have seen), and
then point out at each step the salient features of a
summary from your own example (e.g., identifying for
the audience what you're summarizing, selecting main
ideas, etc.).

Exercise 6D: If it is necessary to do further work on summary,
use the student sample essays in the textbook (see Table of
Contents for page numbers).

Planning an Analysis

Because you have just finished teaching summary, the format of
this essay will not be too difficult for the students.
However, some problems in teaching the analysis of written
material seem inevitable:
- A.   the difference between summarized material (objective,
concise, balanced) and analyzed material (opinionated,
in absolute need of support from facts, examples,
personal experience, and physical description) is

simple in theory and often difficult in practice,
particularly for international students whose cultures
do not demand the use of specific detail in the
presentation of material.

B.   a summary which is clear and concise is generally the
result of close, careful reading; a poor summary often
results in an unfocused analysis. Moreover, the
length of the summary depends on the assignment, the
audience, and the length of the article.

C.   trying to analyze too many aspects of an article can
cause frustration and failure. Like the expository
essays which the students have written in previous
weeks, the response to written material must be
narrowed in topic, planned, and carefully organized.
Students must understand that they will not be able to
respond to all the ideas in the essay; indeed, they
will probably respond to only 3 issues.

D.   the key to writing a successful response, and usually
the biggest problem for the students, is the support.
Some students may have to write a second response
before they understand fully that only specific
detailed support can make their responses
intellectually valid rather than merely emotional
outpourings.

In essence, this essay, like the argumentative essay, seeks to
persuade the readers that the opinions in the response are
valid and viable. For many students, using personal experience
may not seem strong enough for persuasion. Indeed, the
examples of student response to "The Dangers of Television" are
the work of very young writers whose personal experience is the
only proof they have. Older students who have more objective
material to use should certainly be encouraged to do so.
However, if the students choose to use personal experience,
they should qualify their theses and topic sentences with such
phrases as "In my experience," or "The people I know," so that
the personal experience is acceptable within that framework.
You might mention that for international students, personal
experience can be very interesting to their U.S. audience
because their experiences are sometimes quite different from
those of native speakers. The backgrounds of your students
may, therefore, be used as strong evidence. In addition, of
course, general knowledge (facts and examples gathered from
reading, other classes, authorities in the field, etc.) is also
a good form of support, particularly if it is specific and
detailed.

Weak support includes using the article's examples instead of
the writer's own, making very general statements ("Everybody
knows that...," or "obviously the author is wrong about..."),
or attacking the author instead of the ideas in the article
("The author must be a Communist...," or "This author is really
stupid..."). Again, working quite directly with samples in the
textbook, or with others of your choice, in class will help the
students to distinguish between strong and weak support.

Organization of the Summary-Response

The overall organization for the response to written material which is presented first in the text may be initially difficult for students to imitate, but it will help focus and control their essays. Alternate formats, presented later in the chapter, can be used with different critique/review assignments.

NOTE: Be sure to explain again to the students that the sample student paragraphs that respond to "The Dangers of Television" are separate student samples, i.e., each paragraph was written by a different student; there are therefore two introductions, two conclusions, and a variety of types and styles of writing.

Exercise 6E: These two letters (or others that you construct about controversial topics) can be used as an in-class essay, or for small group or collaborative essays.

Ratios of Summary-Analysis Assignments

While this may seem a little too arbitrary and mathematical, students are eager to know the answer to "how much?" Moreover, these rations illustrate the expectations of an academic audience with reference to specific kinds of assignments.

For example, the technical writing assignment (Exercise 6I) is an actual assignment given to first year graduate students in agriculture; it is a typical assignment for a critique (or literature review). Students in scientific fields should have the opportunity to write a summary-analysis using this assignment, though it is considerably more sophisticated in terms of content analysis. Be sure to point out that the components of this assignment are the same as in the summary-response work you have been doing in class. The format is a bit different: a more extended summary with specific details that need to be covered, an analysis that is more objective in its presentation. But the writers must still give their opinions about the validity of the experiment, its place in the entire field, and its usefulness.

Finally, be sure the students understand that this assignment, like the rest of the assignments in the course, will prepare them for a basic format that is used in academic work. Actual assignments may differ in length, expected content, audience, and in some cases, organization. Students must be encouraged to listen carefully to academic writing assignments and to ask intelligent questions about assignments. For instance, in the case of the response to written material, a student could validly ask a question about the relative length between summary and analysis in an assignment, particularly if the professor has not handed out a dittoed assignment but rather has given the assignment verbally in class. You might have your students practice asking viable questions about assignments; that practice will be helpful in doing research in the library as well.

CHAPTER 7: INTRODUCTION TO THE RESEARCH PAPER

In order to teach the students to write research papers, you must be familiar with the library yourself, not only in the field of ESL, but also in the various major fields and fields of interest of your students. Getting to know the librarians can be an enormous help; letting them know that you will help your students if they will teach you often results in immediate assistance, because often the librarians are faced with an international student whom they cannot understand and, worse, who knows virtually nothing about using the library and doing research. Teaching the students to locate and use some of the indexing and abstracting journals, how to ask the librarians to help, and how to ask pertinent questions, will make this section most beneficial to the students.

This chapter begins with the assignment for the research paper, the general format, and sample topics. Notice and point out to the students that student samples are labeled Graduate and Undergraduate.

The students should understand that a research paper is organized and written much as the essays they have written previously in the course. Again, the exercises in this chapter lead the students through the initial steps in preparing to write the research paper. The differences between the research paper and other essays are the research and citation techniques.

Choosing a Topic for Research

The samples of student topics in the textbook are there to show the students the incredible number of topics available to them. Whatever topic a student wishes to explore should be his/her choice (with, of course, your permission once the topic is narrow enough). Students may choose topics in their major fields so that their investigation in the library will help them in later academic work. But if students choose other topics of interest, they should write about that topic in the forms used in their major fields; that is particularly necessary for referencing and footnotes.

In some cases, the expository or argumentative essays students have written previously will become the basis for the research paper. Expanding one paper to complete another assignment, and adding research material to it, is excellent experience for the students. Whatever the student topic, make certain that it is narrow; the tendency of most inexperienced researchers is to say "2000 words! I'd better write about everything!" With this attitude students will drown in material and not be able to finish the research paper on time.

Before the students go to the library, they should have had their topics accepted formally by you; otherwise, they will wander and perhaps get bogged down either because they can find no material, or, more commonly, because they find mounds of it and cannot select. They should also have decided what they need to look for in the library; a simple way of deciding that

is to have them ask questions about their topic: if they don't
have the answers, then they (and you) must decide where they
should go in the library to find those answers.

Preparing to Go to the Library

Following the initial information about selection of the
research topic, this chapter acquaints students with their
academic library. For some students, this section may be
review; for others it will be a new experience. In either
case, "hands-on" exercises are essential; before students can
do library research, they should feel comfortable in the
library. The library research section in POC presumes that the
students have already learned basic library procedures:
  A. using the card catalog and finding a book or
     periodical in the stacks
  B. using general references and The Reader's Guide to
     Periodical Literature.

If the students lack this knowledge, your library will probably
have free handouts, a library tour, and perhaps videotaped
materials available. A map of the library and some discarded
card catalog cards are good in-class materials for the pre-
library lecture(s). Students must then have the opportunity to
have "hands-on" experience. Send them, or better, take them to
the library with a dittoed exercise like the one below:
  1. Go to the loan desk; get a library card.
  2. Listen to the taped material (or obtain the free
     handouts and read them) concerning the use of the card
     catalog, the Reader's Guide, and the serials record
     (the small card catalog for periodicals).
  3. Go to the card catalog; look in the subject area of
     the card catalog and find your chosen research paper
     topic. Indicate on the blanks below 3 citations which
     might help you write your paper. Be sure to include
     all the information about the call number of each
     book.
  4. Go to the Reader's Guide; look up your chosen topic in
     a recent volume. If you can't find your topic, look
     under a more general term. Write below three
     citations which might help you write your paper. Be
     sure to copy all the bibliographic information.
  5. Using the 3 magazines (journals) you wrote down for
     #4, look in the card catalog for magazines (often
     called the serials record). Does this library have
     those magazines? If so, write down the call number
     for each.

NOTE: the exercise above demands some specific vocabulary. A
      list of pertinent library vocabulary, distributed and
      explained in an early class, could help prepare the
      students for their library work.

First-year undergraduates may use only the card catalog and the
Reader's Guide in research, but they should also have the
opportunity to look at other indexing journals that may be of
interest in their future academic careers: Applied Science and
Technology Index, Business Periodicals Index, and Psychological

Abstracts are good examples of indexing/abstracting journals
frequently read by undergraduate researchers.

Descriptors

Students must learn to describe their topics; this section is,
therefore, a vital exercise in general specific and in
identifying a topic. Use student topics and class input to
demonstrate descriptors, and be sure that all students have
adequate descriptors for their topics.

Formats of the Research Paper

Exercise 7G is a good review of the check-out procedure and the
process of finding a book in the card catalog. Your library
may also have an organized list of master's theses, probably
available at the reference desk; ask a librarian for more
information. This exercise allows each student to see what a
major paper looks like. Have the students meet in the library;
help shy and inexperienced students to get started. The
following day, in class, put a grid on the board with the
students' different major fields (see below); then fill in the
grid with information from all the students' completed
exercises.

	Biochemistry	Engineering	Business	Agriculture
abstract: how long?				
number of pages				
organiza- tion				
figures? illustra- tions?				
references? footnotes? biblio- graphy?				
citation format				

It will soon become apparent to the students that major fields
have different formats; the basics are similar (and you can
point that out if everyone has a master's thesis available for

passing around), but the specifics differ, sometimes radically. Demonstrating these differences will also make the students look more closely at the master's thesis they have, and learning about the details of format will help them with their research papers. Most students, regardless of native language, have never looked closely at such things as what is capitalized and where the commas come in citations. Many of the students will consider these details unimportant; you must make the point that indeed, consistency in format is essential in citation.

Another exercise to determine format:
1. Find a periodical or journal in your major field or a field of interest on the library display of current periodicals. Photocopy one article from that journal. Read the article.
2. Look carefully at the verbs: which verb tenses are used, and under what conditions are those tenses used (e.g., is the past tense used in the introduction? is the passive voice used in the article? is the present tense used in the conclusion?).
3. Are the sentences long or short? Count the words in at least ten different sentences from different paragraphs in the article.
4. Are there sub-titles in the article? How is the article divided?
5. Are there footnotes or references in the article? Notice the form: are numbers used to indicate references? are there parentheses within the citations?

Still another way to introduce students to the format of technical writing is to use Consumer Reports. This magazine, published by a non-profit organization (no advertising of consumer products), investigates and evaluates consumer items from stereos to peanut butter. The format and procedure is similar to academic research and reporting: introduction, body (including methods, materials, the process of gathering data, etc.), and conclusion (called "Recommendations"), followed by charts, graphs and tables. Students usually enjoy working with this magazine, particularly if they are going to be making major purchases, because their knowledge of quality in American products is limited. If you spend a class period working with Consumer Reports (you can check out several current back issues from the library), you will no doubt find the students willing to discuss what products they buy and why (What shampoo? What televisions? Why?). As a break from the drudgery of research, students will be very interested in the psychology of advertising in the U.S.

Setting Up Deadlines

Early in the research process, students should understand about your timeline for the research paper. Working backwards from the due date for the final draft of the research paper, set up deadlines for pieces of the assignment; possible deadlines include topic acceptance, reference page(s), outline, introduction, rough draft, and final draft.

CHAPTER 8: LIBRARY RESEARCH

By this time, the students should have chosen their research
topics and perhaps constructed a thesis or even a general
outline for the essay. In a paper of this length, some overall
organizational plan (like an outline) is almost essential.

This chapter gives students the first-hand experience they need
in the process of library research. Students might spend one
class period in the library, the next in class where you might
put topics on the board, identify audiences, and ask peers to
formulate questions they would like answered about a certain
topic.

Be aware of certain misconceptions about research that the
students will have:
A.   most international students have not used a large
     library with open stacks for library research. They
     may not be certain of the process of finding a book
     and they may not know of the existence of abstracting
     journals. Indeed, many native speakers simply go to
     the library and wander (some during their entire
     academic career!) hoping to find an article or two, a
     book or three, to do some research.
B.   Many of the students have used only a couple of old
     books and their major professor's words in writing
     "research" papers in the past; they must understand
     the necessity of using a variety of sources and using
     current research for the academic papers they write in
     the U.S.
C.   some students who have already done research may be
     satisfied with using books "at my home" or in a small
     library located in a building that houses their major
     field department. However, you must persuade them
     that using the main library on campus will provide
     them with a much broader (and in some cases much
     deeper) set of sources for research.

As you go through this chapter, it is essential that you know
more than the students about the library. One way is to peruse
Sheehy's Guide to Reference Books, a huge, thorough, and
helpful volume which is probably located in the reference
section of your library. You might also refer your students to
that volume and suggest that they photocopy the relevant pages
about their major fields.

Learn to use one or two indexing or abstracting journals well
so that you can show the students; then make it clear to the
students that there are dozens of indexing/abstracting journals
and that each operates a little differently. Students will
have to learn to use their indexing and abstracting journals
(i.e., those in their major fields) just as they will learn
"their" place in the library, the place where many of the books
in their major fields are located.

Using Library Materials

As your students begin to assemble "pieces" of their research, you may want to have them bring some of their sources to class and to work on note-taking and the integration of source material in class. Brief conferences with the students, followed by a listing of problems on the board and discussion of possible solutions can prove very helpful for all students.

Gathering Source Materials

Students need to understand the importance of organizing and recording the material they collect about their research topics. There are two ways of carefully collecting material:
1. photocopying: students should photocopy the title page of the article/book (for citation purposes) as well as relevant pages. Highlighting or underlining the material on photocopied pages will make the material immediately available.
2. note-taking: students can use either notecards or a notebook. They must develop strategies to ensure that they collect complete bibliographic data for each entry (including page numbers), that they distinguish between quoted and paraphrased material, and that they can manipulate the pieces of collected material, either by "shuffling" the notecards of by cutting the notebook paper into strips.

Students should work to develop their own coping strategies, and they should have class opportunities to share successes and frustrations.

Plagiarism

Even before the students begin to draft their papers, they need to be warned about the serious problems they may encounter if they copy material (ideas, sentences) that belongs (this is a difficult concept for some cultures) to another writer. As they begin to integrate secondary source material into their papers, students must understand that giving credit to writers (that is, referencing or footnoting material that is not their own) is not only essential to prevent stealing but will also demonstrate to the U.S. academic audience that they are doing broad, deep, valid research.

Despite your lecture on these issues, students may not fully comprehend the problems (and the solutions) of using secondary materials. After all, in many of their previous research projects, using the words of another as their own may have been a form of compliment; therefore, they must learn that differences exist in U.S. academic writing. In addition to having the students read the material concerning documentation (and especially plagiarism), you will need to stress again and again the necessity of quoting and citing material from research sources. Despite going over the citation exercises in the text, only your continued surveillance will prevent wholesale copying without citation from some students.

During the discussion of citation, it is helpful to show the
students how direct quotations, citing of references, and
particularly partial quotations and ellipses can fit into the
text of a research paper. Using student names, you might put
various citations on the board:

A.   In a recent study, Bugren (1988) states...
B.   Results of a recent study (Bugren, 1988) suggest
     that...
C.   S. Bugren, in his recent study of X, demonstrated
     that...
D.   According to S. Bugren (1988), "The use of irradiated
     iodine...destroys the thyroid."
E.   In a series of recent experiments, S. Bugren has
     found that "The use of irradiated iodine...destroys
     the thyroid."[2]

Remember that some of your students will be using footnotes
(either at the bottoms of appropriate pages or on an "Endnote"
page after the text) and Bibliography pages. Other students
will be using author references (e.g., Smith, 1988) or
numerical references, and these may be either chronologically
or alphabetically organized. It is the students'
responsibility to identify their individual formats; it is your
responsibility to check for consistency and correctness.

Exercise 8C

Having your students assemble and draft a reference page even
before they begin to write their papers may seem backwards, but
(a) students need to complete (or almost complete) their
library research early in the process--or else they will spend
more time in the library than they do organizing and writing
the paper, and (b) you need an early check on the library work
they are doing (and how that work is impacting/modifying their
topics). Finally, you will probably discover that despite your
initial work with referencing, half the class will turn in
inappropriate, inconsistent and/or incomplete references.

Computer Searches

If your library has one or more computer search systems, learn
as much about it/them as you can; ask a librarian questions
about cost, the number of data bases available, the process at
your library for use, etc. If possible, you might arrange for
your students to visit a demonstration of a search. Emphasize
that the information you are giving to the students about
computer searches is most likely for later use; there is no
need or time for such a search for the present paper.
Moreover, in some computer systems, only a small number of data
bases exist, so the system may not be helpful for the majority
of students.

However, if the computer system is well developed, the graduate
students in your class in particular should know about it
because it will be of enormous help in their

theses/dissertations. Finally, stress that the computer search only identifies the possible articles; the student must then locate the articles and read them (in some computer searches, you could pay for a computer print-out of the actual articles, but the cost is exorbitant).

Going to the Library

If you are using the library exercises in the text, they should be the first assignment in the library. The dual purpose of these exercises is: to reinforce with practice the theoretical knowledge the students have just learned, and to give each student some initial information about the research paper. Your presence in the library as the students do the exercises is necessary; you will assist the students who are unfamiliar with the library, and more importantly, you will function as a liaison between the students and the librarians by showing the students which questions they can answer themselves (and how) and which they need to ask about for assistance. The confidence needed to ask those questions is vital to the students; very soon the reference librarians will be the only people the students can question.

The first two days in the library are difficult for both you and the students; some students will immediately be self-sufficient, but most will need your help in various parts of the library. Solid preparation before the students go to the library helps, of course; the students will then know where to start, and you will know which students will need most of your help. You might try wearing bright clothes so the students can find you. Try to solve one problem at a time (and teach others waiting for individual help whatever solution you are working on); use the reference librarians, whom you will have warned prior to your visit (i.e., turn the student with a difficult, but precise, problem over to the librarian); group the students who need the same help, and have alternative tasks for students who are waiting for your assistance. And be prepared for native speakers to inch up to any group you're teaching; you'll no doubt be amazed at what the native speakers do not know (and so will your students!).

On the library days, be available and supportive. Individual students will have questions about their research, their outlines, their citations, and their drafts. Having a room in the library where the students can meet initially and then can return to find you is ideal; otherwise, walk the library, attempting to see every student during a class period. As the last week passes, you should have less and less to do with library research and more to do with questions concerning the actual writing of the paper. Some students will "disappear;" the in-class meetings (see below) will ensure that they are keeping up with the rest of the class. Other students will begin to panic for various reasons: not finding enough pertinent material, material being gone from the library, discovering how much material is available and being unable to read it all, etc. Following the schedule of deadlines will be difficult for some, but special encouragement should be given so that these students do finish.

In-Class Meetings

Depending on the timeline for the research paper, have the students do one or two days of work in the library, and then have an in-class meeting to discuss what the students have learned (a helpful learning/sharing experience for all), to answer general questions, and to re-group. Students will need to be reminded that the course time is limited, that they will not be able to do complete research on any topic, that this experience is simply to "get their feet wet," and that the research papers they are writing are quite short. Remind the students again that the indexing and abstracting journals listed in the textbook, as well as the other reference materials, are only samples of the enormous number of publications available in the library.

In another of the in-class meetings, you might have a reference librarian visit the class; this visit can prove very successful if the students prepare beforehand. Have students write three questions about the library concerning their individual research topics. After the librarian has spoken briefly, students should ask questions. Learning to ask appropriate questions is half the battle in a library. Students can try out their questions on you before the arrival of the librarian; probably the most relevant and answerable questions are the more specific ones:

A. "I'm writing a paper about oilseeds as a source of vegetable protein; where should I look to find recent journal articles?"

B. "My paper is about cholesterol. Would a review periodical be helpful? Where can I find one that is relevant?"

C. "My topic is diamond cutting, and I haven't been able to find any recent articles; is there an abstracting or indexing journal that might contain such articles?"

D. "I want to find out about the blood of the camel, but the listings in Chemical Abstracts are too difficult for me. Is there another indexing or abstracting journal which contains entries that are easier to read?"

E. "I'm writing about injuries in soccer. The Reader's Guide articles that I've found don't have any data. Where can I find some?"

Teaching the students to ask pertinent questions that are focused and specific will help them immeasurably in later library work, so even if the librarian doesn't come to class to answer questions, the students should practice asking them.

CHAPTER 9: WRITING THE RESEARCH PAPER

This is the week in which the students complete their research, plan their papers, and begin writing the rough drafts. Some students will complete their rough drafts; others will begin to fall behind. You will be the monitor, the editor, the encourager, and the helper both in the process of research and in the process of organizing and writing the rough drafts. Remind the students of the deadlines. Perhaps the final draft of the research paper can serve as the final examination, which will give the students a little extra time. Time becomes increasingly important as the deadlines grow near, and some students may be more frustrated than others. But this kind of assignment is very like academic assignments they will have later, so you simply have to keep their collective chins up.

You might set up a schedule for conferences to see outlines and rough drafts, and to discuss writing problems. If you have a classroom available for your class in the library, have conferences there; if not, perhaps there is a single place in the library where students can find you for conferences, or you can conference in the classroom. Even at these conferences, you will continue to exhort the students to finish their research, to finish their rough drafts, and to meet the deadline for the final draft.

Techniques for Using Source Materials

This section gives students many examples of integrating source material with their own ideas. Encourage the students to experiment with different "lead-ins," and use individual problems from student papers to demonstrate solutions. Review the differences in citation formats in different fields, and the need for absolute consistency in whatever form the student chooses. Many students will still not be very perceptive about commas, indentation, and the like, but they need to be sensitive to these small points if their citations are to be correct.

If students have basic questions to ask you during class or during individual conferences concerning citation or organization, refer them either to the master's thesis exercise they completed or to the sample research paper in the textbook. If the students follow the format of "their" master's theses, they can be assured that their papers will be acceptable to academic readers because the papers will fulfill the expectations of those professors. However, if an undergraduate who is undecided about a major field asks for help, have him/her use the format of the textbook research sample if s/he is scientifically or technically oriented, or introduce him/her to the APA (American Psychological Association) Style Sheet (available in most academic bookstores) if s/he is in the humanities or social sciences. Another good source of citation is the Biology Editors Style Sheet which is used by many fields of science.

NOTE: The Twelve Common Problems (and Solutions) list can
         provide an overview of students' experiences and/or a
         review of the processes involved in writing a research
         paper.

The Abstract

The abstract is a form of summary; it is written last (although
it appears even before the introduction!) because it summarizes
the beginning, the middle, ad the end of the research paper.
You will need to stress the differences between the abstract
and the introduction for your students; photocopying half a
dozen abstracts from diverse journals and examining those
abstracts in class will be helpful. You might also select
certain structural aspects of the abstract to stress:

```
         This research    project    examines...
                          study      discusses
                          paper

         X was    studied...
                  investigated

         Experiments  show (showed)...
         Analysis shows (showed)...

         X is described as...
         X, Y, and Z were studied extensively...
         X has been measured...

Note the use of passive voice with no personal
pronouns and the complexity of sentence structures.
```


Student Samples

The final section of this chapter contains a variety of samples
to study, imitate, or adapt for student research papers.
Please notice that each "page" has been reduced to a box in
order to conserve space; explain that the title page, for
example, will be a separate page in the final draft of the
research paper. If you have taught the research paper before
and have photocopies of previous student research papers, you
might allow your students to peruse such papers.

Teachers of this class have found it helpful to have their
students turn in completed first drafts about a week before the
final drafts are due. This process keeps students focused on
the timeline, and it allows teachers to discover last-minute
problems before the final draft.

As the due date for final drafts approaches, remind the
students that you want all of their "garbage" (their notes,
their rough draft, etc.) as well as the photocopied and note-

taking materials they used as they wrote their papers. This gives you a check system; if a student has copied material, you will be able to find the source. Indicate that you will return all the materials after you have evaluated their final drafts.

The final in-class period can be spent sharing each other's research papers. Students should read at least two; even if they don't understand all of what they read, the positive feedback of seeing finished papers, of having an audience, and of hearing from that audience, is a very pleasant way to end the class.

NOTE: As the class draws to an end, and often after the class has ended, you may be contacted by graduate students and/or professors in various fields who are interested in knowing about your research writing process. It is valuable to have sample research papers written by the students you have had to show to these inquirers. Photocopy the papers which have most closely followed the formats of master's theses; photocopy salient parts of other research papers that you can use in future classes as additional student samples. And if students have asked to do an alternate form of research (e.g., a protocol for a master's thesis, a grant proposal), keep the results for future reference.

CHAPTER 10: GRAMMATICAL EXPLANATIONS AND EXERCISES

Just as the research section of the textbook can be cut or
extended as time and need dictate, this chapter can be used
either as a series of diagnostic exercises or in a more lengthy
manner (with supplemental materials from your students'
writing). This chapter concerns problems most often faced by
ESL writing students. It is not an orderly, progressive,
linguistically based section; rather, it seeks to explain, in
the simplest and most efficient manner possible, what specific
errors exist and how to correct them. Rules and exceptions to
rules which are not generally encountered in expository or
argumentative prose are excluded, and errors which individual
students might have difficulty with are left to individual
remedial work assigned by you, either from the books cited in
Chapter 10, or in books of your choice. The suggested
textbooks deal in detail with specific grammatical problems and
have proved useful to teachers of this course in the past.

The explanations and exercises should probably be worked with
in class only when the majority of students need the work,
particularly on those days when you hand back student writing
and assign revisions. The section on verb tense, for example,
is very limited, and students who do the exercises should
understand that if they make many errors, they should spend
additional time studying verb tenses, perhaps in Mastering
American English.

The sentence structure exercises may be especially valuable for
students who consistently write comma-spliced sentences; you
might encourage students to thoroughly learn what an
independent clause is and then try to limit their sentences to
a maximum of three independent clauses, using only one semi-
colon and only one comma (+ a short word) before using a
period. Incidentally, the "short" and "long" word approach has
been a successful learning device for teachers of this course.

At various times in this Teacher's Manual, exercises in Chapter
10 have been suggested for use; the sentence combining
exercises, for example, may be used when teaching abstracts or
when doing revisions. For many students who have not had
sentence combining before, this section can provide an insight
into the language, an understanding that English is not a
childish, subject-verb-object language after all.

The exercises on precision in diction can be used simply as
review of previously learned material or as a review of the
straightforwardness of U.S. academic prose. In some cases,
students may argue that the most elaborate sentences (in
English, more wordy) are more acceptable, but you will have to
stress that conciseness and precision are the foundations of
U.S. academic prose.

THE APPENDIX

The Resume

This appendix may be an assigned part of the course, perhaps at
the beginning of the course or with the section on summary. A
resume can be explained as a summary of a person's life,
qualifications, goals and interests; its purpose is to convince
an employer to invite the writer for an interview.

If you use this assignment at the beginning of the course,
students can write about themselves in this format and then
exchange resumes with other students; both the class members
and the teacher get to know the students better. Writing
resumes in English may initiate class discussion that compares
and contrasts the kinds of resumes prepared in other cultures.

Writing a resume requires knowledge of the audience, and, in
English, great selection and precision, because brevity, focus,
and clarity are prized. Moreover, the information on the
resume, which generally is just a single page, must be arranged
and selected with the audience in mind. Each of the sample
resumes in the textbook follows a slightly different format;
students may choose what "look" appeals to them and follow it.
You might ask the students what audience they think the
textbook samples were designed for. Writing a resume can be
not only a class introduction for the students, but, in some
cases at least, an utterly practical assignment.

The Business Letter

Very likely, this part of the appendix will be used for review;
presumably, most of the students know how to write a formal
letter. However, this business letter reflects the tone of
many English business letters: it is very direct, quite
straightforward, and, perhaps just as important, speaks
positively about the writer. Many students will be reticent
about "selling" themselves, but for those who are applying for
school admission or a job, that aspect of U.S. business letter
writing is important.